# Madame Alexander's
# Ladies of Fashion

*by*

*Marjorie Victoria Sturges Uhl*

**Cover Photo: Madame Alexander**
**Doll: Cissy/Lissy**

**Edited By:**
**Wayne Shively**
**Patricia R. Smith**
**Barbara Faulkner**

**Collector Books**
**P.O. Box 3009**
**Paducah, Kentucky   42001**

# DEDICATION

The dedication of this book has been a very hard task for me. There are a great many that I should and quietly do thank, but the following are uppermost in importance.

To Madame Alexander, I dedicate this book as a lasting testimony to her own greatness of creative ability.

To Dwight Smith for the help of making slides from photos for me.

To Patricia Smith for her constant encouragement and guidance.

To my Father and Mother, Alfred and Beatrice Sturges, whom I love very much.

To my husband, Theodore B. Uhl, a very warm and special thank you.

# CREDITS

All photographs by Frank O'Rear, Genelli Studio, Sioux City, Iowa, except the following:

Cover photo of Madame Alexander: Copy by Dwight F. Smith

Roberta Lago: By Ted Long, Seattle, Wash.

Sargent Collection: By Jeri Alterman, N.Y.

Connie Bean. By Roy Bean. Slide by Dwight F. Smith

Memory Brengle: By herself. Slide by Dwight F. Smith

Charmaine Shields: By herself. Slides by Dwight F. Smith

Marian Knox, Marjorie Biggs and Velma Gee, also by Frank O'Rear

**Additional Copies of This Book May Be Ordered From:**

**COLLECTOR BOOKS**
**P. O. Box 3009**
**Paducah, Kentucky 42001**

or

**Marjorie Uhl**
**811 Souix Ave.**
**Mapleton, Iowa 51034**

**$19.95 Plus $1.00 for Postage**

Copyright: Marjorie Uhl, Bill Schroeder 1979
Reprinted 1982
ISBN: 0-89145 100-5

**Printed by Taylor Publishing Company, Dallas, Texas**

# CONTENTS

# A SALUTE TO MADAME ALEXANDER

Madame Alexander, we salute you for your great creative ability that has given us the most beautiful dolls of this century! Not only have you given us hundreds of dolls dressed in the fashions of today, but you have brought to the collector wonderful moments of history by costuming in the fashions of yesteryear. You have always insisted in using the finest of materials and workmanship, of which we can all be justly proud. Your almost unbelievably beautiful children stand proudly in the collections of today, and will continue into the hands of our children's children, to stand proudly before the future declaring your own beauty and creative ability. It is through your dolls that you will achieve life forever, for you will never be forgotten.

We can tell, from your dolls, that you delight in the joys of others. You have earned every word of praise through your endeavor to give of yourself through your creations, and it is because of this that we salute you.

# COLLECTING MADAME ALEXANDER DOLLS

Collecting dolls has been much more than a hobby for me. When my family was raised, I found I had donated myself so totally to that task that I had no main interests in my life after the children grew up and left home. Collecting dolls and meeting friends through dolls has been a great diversion from the loneliness of missing the children.

Doll collecting can be a rewarding experience, no matter the collector's age. If you are a young collector, the addition of one doll every six months can be an event to look forward to with great joy. If retired, or alone, many happy hours can be spent building your collection. The lucky collectors are the ones that can share collecting with a friend or a loved one, for like other good things in life, the sharing is the pleasant experience. Even if the husband or friend collects other items instead of dolls, both can attend antique shows and sales, flea markets, garage sales, etc. and share the joy of each other's discoveries. I have talked and visited with husband and wife doll collectors, and find these people are indeed lucky, for one point stands out, and that is that a happy wife makes for a happy life.

I would like to jot down helps and hints that I have found through my collecting of dolls, in the hopes that what I have learned may be of interest to you, as well as perhaps helping a novice collector.

You may be able to place an available doll in lay-a-way when you are short of funds. This privilege is often extended to interested buyers. I want to add, however, it is just that, a privilege and an inconvenience to the dealer, so be fair with her. Be prompt with payments and pay off the balance as quickly as possible. If a crisis should arise and you need a refund, or are willing to take another doll for money you have paid down . . . talk to the dealer about it, I'm sure she will find a solution agreeable to both of you.

One important thing to know and always remember is to deal with only those with whom you know to have a reliable reputation. Buy from dealers who give a five day return privilege. It is impossible to return a doll in three days, so stay clear of dealers who only offer three days as this is the same as no return privilege. If you do not mind gambling and taking a chance, then stay very clear of dealers advertising no return privileges.

It is almost impossible to do business by mail in less than five days, therefore you need that period in which to culminate the deal. One point which is very important is not to let your excitement cloud your good judgement. Look the doll over carefully, then if you decide to return her, do it at once. Examine the doll with care to see if she is cracked. (Hard plastic and vinyl Cissys).

Cissys have a tendency to crack in the seams between the legs and under the ear, on the seams that extend down to the edge of the head. Lissy dolls tend to crack around the ears. If any of these dolls are strung too tightly it will, in time, cause the seam under the ears to crack open. If you think your doll is strung too tightly it is an easy thing to re-string her. What you will need is patience and a long afghan crochet hook. I sometimes use a silk stocking to loop through the rubber band and pull it through the body. But, this bears repeating, examine the doll as soon as you receive her. I have bought dolls, and was so excited about the purchase that I didn't take time to look, only later to discover that I had bought a damaged doll.

If you are buying a doll through an advertisement in a publication, and you call to reserve that doll only to find later that you do not want it, or are unable to buy it, call and tell the seller. You made the call to buy, you can make the second call to cancel. The dealer will understand better if you phone right away than she would a week later when she receives a letter from you saying you do not want the doll. This not getting a doll is a two way street. I have been offered dolls only to have them sold to someone else who offered more, or because the person changed their mind about selling the doll. This is unfortunate and can cause hard feelings, but you have to accept these things and continue to enjoy your hobby without malice. I hope in the future we can have a reference sheet of reliable dealers (and collectors) from whom we can buy. The majority of dealers and collectors are honest and will bend over backwards to straighten out a misunderstanding.

There are many reasons a dealer may turn "bad" and it would take a book unto itself to explain this fact. The best guideline to follow is if once burned, don't invite pain by sticking your hand into the same fire. I have learned this from experience and will sight you one example: I purchased a doll, by phone, that I had been looking for for years and the party I bought from knowing this, charged me an abnormal price for the doll. I paid, so the fault with the price of the doll is no one's but my own. I was told the doll was "tissue mint" (meaning unplayed with) and upon receiving the doll I had hunted years for, I found it to be dirty, and the clothes were on the wrong doll. I re-called immediately and was told the money had been spent to buy three other dolls I had been looking for, which had been purchased for me, and my money, therefore could not be refunded. I accepted this form of blackmail and kept the doll beyond the five days return privilege. I did not receive the other three dolls, which were sold to another collector, and am stuck with a very expensive non-mint doll. This particular incident hurt me deeply, but I also learned a great lesson from it. Do not let yourself become so avid to add to your own collection that you allow the greed of unethical dealers take advantage of you.

I love Alexander dolls and am not a dealer, but like many others, I have sold from my own collection. I have had to buy entire collections to get the few dolls that I really wanted and have had to sell the duplicates, or dolls that I did not really want.

Appreciate doll reference books. They are made up with a great deal of hard work. Reference books are priceless when it comes to decisions about which dolls are going to be desirable to you. In these books you generally can see the picture of the doll you may be wondering about and you can actually make up your mind if you want to try and find a particular doll to add to your collection, or not. Some dolls seem to "turn on" different people and the old saying "Beauty is in the eye of the beholder" is never more true than in the collecting of dolls. Some of these reference books are guides to prices and can be very helpful, but remember they are GUIDES only and will give you an *area* of price range you can expect to have to pay for a certain doll.

If you are looking to dolls as an investment only, you are wasting your time and money. If you are looking for a sound investment take your money to the bank. If you are looking for enjoyment and fun, then invest in dolls. Who knows, perhaps you will leave your grandchildren a fortune in dolls . . . and then again, you just may leave them the best darn doll collection in the country and, or embark them on a joyful pastime, such as you have enjoyed. Remember that the dolls will outlive all of us, have fun and enjoy them while you are on this good earth. I put great value and love on many of the dolls in my collection. Some are as rare as the rarest of French bisque, and I am sure that I enjoy them as much.

Let's talk about the word "mint" and dolls in original boxes. A mint doll/original box should be in PERFECT condition, which is often referred to as "tissue mint". A near mint doll is one without its original box and possibly a tiny bit soiled. She must have all her original clothing and any jewelry that may have come with her. Actually, very few dolls have their original boxes, plus many times a store clerk was in a hurry and put the wrong doll in the wrong box.

With the Cissy, Lissy and Elise dolls, jewelry can be questionable because it could be purchased separately and often was added by the original owner. The Alexander company catalogues sometimes list certain pieces of jewelry, but these were printed ahead of actual production of the dolls, and sometimes the dolls were not produced with the items listed.

If you should wash a doll's garment be sure to press it with care or have a good dry cleaner do it for you. If taken to a cleaner, be sure to inform them of the age of the garment since he will be able to make an intelligent decision about the solutions he uses on that certain material. Be careful not to allow them to press creases in the sleeves which take away from the beauty of the doll's clothing. If you press the sleeve yourself, stuff it with tissue or cloth, being careful not to leave a ridge inside so that when you put the pressure of the iron, that it leaves a crease. Always turn taffeta inside out to press and use a cool iron. Satin should be dry cleaned, if possible. Many of you like to re-dress your dolls and, if so, store their clothing, as these have much value, as they are original garments. And, let me add, even if you think you will never sell a re-dressed doll, do not make the mistake of selling her clothes.

The really super, mint Alexander dolls do not come into collections easily and often. So that we can continue to collect, we sometimes will buy "lesser" dolls and do so because we want to. It is fun to collect dolls, and I know that the collecting of Madame Alexander dolls is especially rewarding and I wish you all the luck you need to achieve the collecting goals you have placed on yourself.

Margaret

Maggie
Mixup

CoCo

Maggie

Jacqueline

Lissy

**Cissy
Shiny Finish**

**Cissy
Bisque Like**

**Cissy
Matte Finish**

**Cissette**

Elise, Marybel Head, Hard Plastic, Vinyl and Today's
Head

**Polly**

22″ . . . "JUDY" . . . All composition, wig rolled to top and very elaborate gown with inset, pinch-pleated flowers at hem of skirt. (Wendy). 1946. One of the portrait series and inspired by Judy from the movie "Meet Me in St. Louis". A Margaret O'Brien doll was also dressed for this movie in 1946. Although the movie debut was 1944-45; it re-opened in N.Y. during 1946.

22" — Composition Princess Flavia. 1946 Gown of white patterned satin, with lace insert in skirt. Painted lashes in corner of eyes, and hand painted features with blue eyeshadow, and blue eyes. A childhood classic character, Princess Flavia was portrayed in movie by Madeline Carroll in "Prisoner of Zenda." Doll is unmarked. Store tag inside of dress reads: (Bullock's Wilshire) $75.00 (Wendy).

22" June Bride. Composition. Gown is of satin sweetheart neckline. Full long puffed sleeves. Embroidered flowers near hemline. Veil cascades to floor and in full train behind our bride. 1946 Wendy.

22" Composition "Godey" of Portrait Series of 1946. Dressed in pink taffeta and beige lace. High styled hat with flower trim. Painted features. Eye lashes hand painted in corners. Brown eyes. (Wendy)

22" Composition bride from 1947 "Royal Wedding". Dress is of white organdy with full puffed sleeves bracelet length. The skirt is fashioned with most unusual detail. Cut on princess lines, and with 3 full circles of matching organdy sewn into each seam and trimmed with lace. Painted features, gray eyeshadow with painted eye lashes in corner and blue eyes. She wears 4 leaf clover tag, long wavy mohair wig, a ring, pearls in necklace, and earrings. (Wendy)

14" Godey Group. 1950 all hard plastic. *From left to right* — Godey lady dressed in green felt bonnet, white ruffled tulle trim inside hat, gold and black braid around edge, feathers and black lace around crown. Her dress is of pink taffeta with black lace trim on hemline, and on edge of bustle in back. She wears a 4 leaf clover wrist tag reading, "Godey Lady". Made of finest plastic. Can be washed.

Opposite side reads: Madame Alexander all rights reserved. Our lady wears pink pantaloons, pink full slip. She has blue eyes. Dress tag reads "Godey Lady". Madame Alexander. New York U.S.A. All rights reserved. (Wendy). *Second from left* — "Godey Lady" in orange taffeta. *Third from left* — Godey Man. Suit tag reads: Madame Alexander, New York, N.Y. U.S.A. (Maggie). *Fourth* — Bride. Dress tag reads: "Godey Lady". New York, New York, U.S.A. (Wendy) *Fifth from left* — Godey Lady dressed in bright pink. Wendy.

1953, Beaux Arts Creations. Fulfilling the fondest wish of every little girl, and of collectors young in heart. Eighteen inches tall, all hard plastic, walkers. #2025, Queen Elizabeth in white gown, blue sash of the garter and long, velvet robe. #2020B, Princess Margaret Rose in a blush pink faille taffeta, #2020C, petal pink satin and a long brocaded satin coat of blue. #2020D, gown of aqua taffeta with nylon net stole. #2020E, chartreuse taffeta with sash of forest green taffeta. #2028, white satin ball gown with red taffeta evening cape.

18″ — 1953 Beaux Arts Creations. #2025 Queen Elizabeth looking regal indeed wearing her white brocade court gown and blue sash of the garter. Her long purple velvet robe has a cape and border of white fur (felt) and gold braid. Her tiara, earrings and bracelet are jeweled. She wears long, white gloves. Her escort, of course, is Prince Philip looking handsome in his tux. (Both — Margaret) 1953.

18″ — 2020B Princess Margaret Rose wearing a court gown of blush-pink faille taffeta decorated with sequins. Her tiara and bracelet are rhinestone and ruby. Her earrings and necklace are of pearls. Her undergarments consist of a full hoop petticoat of pink taffeta, nylon stockings, and pink satin slippers. (Margaret) 1953.

1953: 18″ Glamour Girls (Walker) Hat box and hoop skirts with attached panties are a part of each girl's costume.

18″ — 2001A Edwardian. Bright pink embossed cotton, black taffeta and lace bonnet with pink ostrich feather. She has ash-blonde hair and blue eyes. (Margaret) 1953.

18″ — #2001B — Blue Danube, long dress of bright-blue print with green leaves and rosebuds trimmed with lace. Her hat is made entirely of lace with two rows of veil lace framing her face. She has rosebuds tucked in over each ear, white gloves, blue eyes and auburn red hair. (Maggie) 1953.

18" — 2001C Picnic Day, green leaves on strawberry pink make up this polished print. A yellow sash of satin at waist forms a small bustle tie in back. Warm brown hair and brown eyes. (Margaret) 1953

18" — #2001C This doll is identical in every detail to Picnic Day except that background of print is blue instead of pink. (Margaret) 1953.

18″ — #2010A Godey Lady wears a beautiful gown with high rise of red taffeta up into the bodice forming an empire waist dress. The top bodice and sleeves are of white taffeta. Grey fur cloth cape-stole has neckline trimmed with red taffeta. (Maggie) 1953

18" — #2010B — Civil War. White taffeta dress with scoop neckline trimmed with lace. Red rose buds cascade down the front of the dress. Red rosebuds encircle the crown of her large sheer picture hat and pick up the color of her cheeks and lips. Her hair and eyes are brown. (Margaret) 1953.

18″ — #2010C — Victorian. Skirt and sleeves of this gown are made of pink taffeta with bodice and sleeve trim of black velvet. The bonnet is of stiff, black net with an open crown trimmed with 3 rows of black lace over face and a row of trim around back of bonnet. Her tie is black tuile, and she wears a garland of roses at her waist and in her hair. (Maggie) 1953.

18″ — #2020A Queen Elizabeth II is wearing a white brocade gown with blue sash and garter, jeweled tiara, earrings and a rhinestone bracelet. (Margaret) 1953

18″ — WENDY BRIDE — 1953/came with 2 style veils. All hard plastic, Walker. She wears a white taffeta dress with overlay of tulle matching sleeves. The full-length veil is held by a complete circle of field flowers. She has brown hair and blue eyes and carries her bridal bouquet with pride. (Margaret)

1954, "Me and My Shadow," 18-inch, hard plastic walkers. Seven dolls — four have miniature matching portraits seven and one-half inches tall and using the Wendy Ann doll.

18″ — 1954, "Me and My Shadow" — #2030C Victoria and miniature #0030C, 7½″ Victoria. 1850 costume of slate-blue taffeta with side-panniers. The side drapery is edged with narrow, white silk braid. The hat is of stiff, white lace trimmed with a topknot of roses and forget-me-nots and tied with a sheer pink ribbon. Reticule (small bag) adds a touch of color. (Maggie) Sargent Collection

7½″ 1954, "Me and My Shadow" — #2035D, Mary Louise. No photo available of larger doll. Mary Louise is dressed in a gown fitting the Gody period. The gown is faille taffeta the color of burnt sugar, her hat is olive-green wool felt and matches the color in her jacket. Yellow kid gloves. (Cissy) Sargent Collection.

18″ — #2035E, 1954, "Me and My Shadow" — Elaine. Garden party dress of pale-blue organdy with rows of val lace. Underneath she wears a dress of pink taffeta, a hoop skirt, and matching panties. The puffed sleeves and round neckline are outlined with pearls. She has a blue-satin sash, a picture hat and pink satin slippers. Doll pictured is minus the pink taffeta dress. (Cissy) Sargent Collection.

18″ — #2030A, 1954, "Me and My Shadow" Queen is same as Glamour Girl Walker of 1953 except for addition of waist-length fur cloth cape. (Margaret)

18″ — "Me and My Shadow" — 1954, #2015 A. Blue Danube. A dancing gown of pale blue taffeta with a side drapery of striped blue and gold taffeta, tiny gold coronet, gold necklace and jeweled bracelets. (Cissy) Sargent Collection.

18″ — #2030B 1954 "Me and My Shadow". Cherie. She wears a heavy white satin gown caught up with bright-pink roses. Her floor-length opera coat of Goya pink taffeta is lined and fastened at the neck with a large bow. The doll pictured is minus the rose-trimmed satin bag. She wears roses in her hair. (Maggie) Sargent Collection.

18" "Lady Churchill and Sir Winston Churchill" All hard plastic walkers 1953. Lady Churchill is wearing a pink satin coat with painted dots of matching color. Her coat is trimmed with rhinestones in 4 rows around neckline. Her gown is of the same material and color. She wears a ring, rhinestone earrings, and a jeweled tiara. She carries a small matching handbag. (Margaret).

## CISSY

Cissy was introduced in 1954 and used extensively through 1962. She is 20″ to 21″ tall with a young adult figure with high heel feet, jointed knees and elbows and came as a walker and non walker. During the 1950's this doll was used in a great many Yardley of London magazine ads. Cissy proved to be one of the most successful dolls manufactured by Alexander Doll Co.

Many outfits not shown in the company catalogs were made for this doll, and to date, there are known to be 10 outfits for 1955, 14 in 1956, 15 in 1957, 23 in 1958 and 3 in 1959. This does not mean that that is all that were released for this doll as surprises keep happening and new discoveries are made all the time.

A collector could attempt to gather in only Cissys and the end result would be a beautiful collection of dolls. The quality of the doll's clothes are the best, including corsets, lace edged panties, fancy shoes, hats, gloves, lace chemise and jewelry, plus the materials used for her outfits was the finest.

Cissy dolls came with blonde, ash blonde, brunette and red hair. I have never seen a Cissy with any color of eyes but blue. The wig styles vary from the plain to the most fancy, which includes braided or twisted hairdos. The brunettes are the hardest to find with mint hairdo and all eyelashes.

Some of the Cissys, pictured in this book, are extremely rare and, I personally, do not believe many dolls were made in these exceptional outfits. At one time I had over 60 Cissys in my personal collection with no two alike and I have tried to present as many of them as possible in this book.

The collecting of these dolls to photograph has been a joy, at times frustrating, and in some cases very expensive, to say the least. It has been an experience into the past, for, remembering that Cissy's destiny was to bring happiness to little girls, she has also brought many hours of happiness to adult collectors.

One more point is that Cissy was the best dressed young lady of her day and it would be impossible to tell if the outfit your Cissy is wearing is the outfit she was bought in.

A glorious career from 1955 through 1962, as a teenager to a young adult, modeling high fashions created by Madame Alexander. Cissy, this is your life!

20″ — #2084. 1955. Cissy looking pretty in a navy-blue taffeta dress made with a long torso waist, featuring a very full waist and tiny sleeves. On her brunette hair she wears a straw hat with cornflower blue trim, field flowers and veil. Open toe shoes and silk stockings.

20″ — #2083. 1955. Cissy wearing a most striking combination of fire-red polished cotton dress and a red and white striped shirt worn over a white ruffled cancan. High heels and a natural straw hat.

20″ — #2097. 1955. Blue-eyed, dark-brown hair Cissy models a blue satin gown with cap sleeves, and scoop neckline. Front panel decorated with blue sapphires and catching the corner of the cap sleeve in front is the highlight of her gown. A third large sapphire on center at neckline. Small stones grace the front of her dress and enhance the beauty of the silver and white braid trim forming the design in the panel. She wears a three-rhinestone ring and carries an ostrich-feather fan. Her coronet is of flowers and jewels.

20″ — #2095. 1955. Cissy wearing summer gown of sheer-white organdy, trimmed with rows of lace and rosebuds. Her sash and hand bag are red satin. Her large picture hat is of white straw lace which is trimmed with red ribbon and small, red velvet flowers. She wears a ruby ring.

20″ — #2099. 1955. Queen Elizabeth wears white brocade with blue garter sash and star. Her tiara, earrings and bracelet are jeweled with rhinestones and rubies. She wears long, white gloves. The 1956 — #2042 Queen was this same doll.

20″ — #2100. 1955. Cissy modeling a beautiful torso-fitting gown of mauve taffeta. This gown is meticulously made with a cellophane tape cleverly braided into a pink braid to decorate the neckline edge. The trim of her skirt circles over a full flounce and is gold, mauve and blue caught on both sides with a gold circle featuring a center of five pearls. Double drop pearl earrings, wide rhinestone and gold bracelet. (The Cissy in photo wears a lavender and pearl necklace put on by the lady from whom I purchased it.)

20″ — 1956. Cissy goes to a fashion parade.

20″ — # 2025. 1956. Blonde, blue-eyed Cissy goes dancing in a ballerina-length dress of nylon tulle over soft pink taffeta. Bodice is of lace over taffeta with a tiny drop sleeve. Skirt of tulle over taffeta forming unpressed pleats. She wears a pink sash at dropped waistline which features a spray of pink flowers. Gold sling back shoes, stockings, pearl earrings and a ring. In her hair she wears a sprig of flowers to draw attention to tiny curls in a cluster at crown of her head.

#2020. 1956. (Not shown in catalogue) Cissy elaborately dressed in white silk pongee with overlay of embroidered silk pongee. Her strapless gown is trimmed with a heart-shaped neckline and a white tulle ruffle matching the deep tulle flounce at the bottom of her gown. Over her shoulders she wears a matching stole and at her waistline is a large, red rose. She wears cameo earrings, a single stone necklace and a solitare ring. Cissy has a special hairdo of tiny curls at the crown of the head. She has a full, white taffeta slip, a lace chemise, stockings, and gold sandals.

#2041. 1956. Ball gown of pink satin worn over a full petticoat of taffeta. She has a pink satin lined shoulder shrug of gray orlon nutria and jeweled earrings.

20″ — #2025 — Cissy wearing a beautiful lavender satin or evening sheath dress with detachable skirt. She wears an open-crown nylon net hat with three-tiered ruffles and trimmed with flowers and a lavender satin ribbon. She wears silver sandals, a silver and rhinestone bracelet, flowers at the neckline, and she carries a small handbag. 1956

20″ — #2025. Cissy wearing a beautiful blue satin afternoon or evening sheath dress with detachable skirt. She wears an open-crown nylon net hat with three-tiered ruffles and trimmed with flowers and a pink satin ribbon. She wears silver sandals, a silver and rhinestone bracelet, flowers at the neckline, and she carries a small handbag. 1956. Cissy is standing beside a Madame Alexander box of yellow.

20″ — #2030. 1956. Blonde, blue-eyed Cissy wearing a full-length bridesmaid's gown of nylon tulle. Her long-waisted gown has pleated nylon tulle over taffeta. The bodice is brought alive with glittering silver threads. Tiny rhinestones are at each corner of the cap sleeve. Her narrow hat of tulle extends across the crown of her head and is pinned at each side with a sprig of flowers. She wears silver sling-back pumps, and carries a bridal bouquet of tiny flowers. She wears a blue sapphire ring.

20″ — 1956. #2035. Blonde Cissy wearing a dress of baby blue organdy, featuring a full skirt of three tiers trimmed with rosebuds and a matching organdy sash. Her large picture hat is decorated with baby rosebuds and is tied under her chin framing her pretty face. She will look her loveliest at a garden party.

20″ — 1956. #2036. Dress in catalogue is pink. This dress is identical to #2036 Cissy wearing a long torso gown of bright red. A cummerbund waist cascades down to form a side drapery caught up by a rhinestone jeweled pin. Pearl earrings, flowers in her hair, and evening bag complete her costume. (Evening bag and flowers missing.)

20″ — #2043. 1956. Cissy wears a black velvet torso gown with a nylon tulle flounce from knees to floor. Satin or taffeta lines the gown at shoulders. Pink rose-buds trim the gown at shoulders and bring attention to the flounce.

20" — #2040. 1956. Red-headed Cissy bride wearing a white gown of pleated nylon tulle over taffeta. Her pink sash is pulled through loops of pearls and tied in back leaving floor-length streamers. Her veil is floor-length caught up with a Medici cap of tulle fastened on each side by white field flowers and pink buds. She wears a diamond ring and carries a bridal bouquet. The neckline of her dress is trimmed with pearls.

20″ — #2012. 1956. Cissy wearing a rose taffeta dress, elbow-length sleeves, and featuring a drop waistline. The neck of her dress forms a V with gathers at the bustline. She wears a taffeta cancan petticoat, nylon stockings and strap shoes, and a darling pill box hat.

20″ — #2014. 1956. Cissy steps out for an afternoon of shopping in a bright pink-striped, cotton shirt-waist dress. She wears a tiny, black, velvet hat, and carries a shiny hat box. A black bow and a black contour belt add to the charm of her outfit. She wears black, high-heeled sandals, nylons, and a white cancan petticoat.

20″ — #2017. 1956. Cissy wearing a most becoming teal blue taffeta dress with dropped waistline, and featuring a small bolero of black velvet. Her tiny hat of black velvet and flowers is her crowning glory. She wears a rhinestone bracelet, afternoon bag, sling-back shoes and stockings.

20″ Cissy wearing a rose colored coat, a natural straw hat trimmed with flowers, and a red satin ribbon. Her dress is a voile print. Around her waist she wears a velvet belt. She wears a rick-rack trimmed slip, nylon panties, stockings, and high heeled shoes.

20″ — #2019. 1956. Cissy, wearing a red-dotted, swiss organdy shirtwaist dress with a wide red ribbon belt and a straw hat with flowers and veil. High-heeled sling-back shoes, and stockings complete her costume. She has on a full crinoline slip with ruffles of ribbon and net and she carries a hat box.

20″ — #2020. 1956. Cissy in a gold, satin theater dress with matching coat. She wears a tiny tulle hat, beads at her neck, high-heeled sandals, nylon stockings, and carries a small pocket book.

18" — 1892 — 1956 (Story Princess). Jointed at elbows and knees. Her wand is plastic with Rhinestone. She has rubies in her crown. She wears pantaloons and silver plat shoes. Her dress is Rose Net with flowers tucked in folds of skirt. Courtesy — Roberta Lago

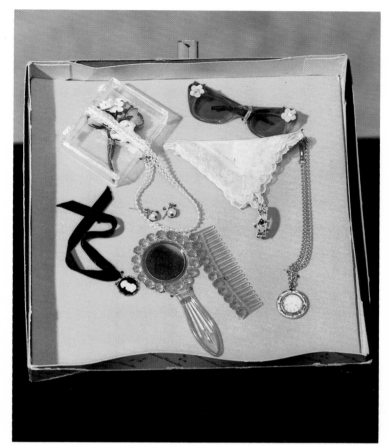

Accessories sold for Cissy, #22-90. Price on box reads: $.75. (Courtesy Marge Meisinger)

Cissy modeling a black chemise, and a corselet. She is holding a corset with attached pantie, and a bra. They wear mules on their feet. Mules are a type of slipper worn with a house coat or nightie, much like bedroom slippers of today. These are items that were sold separately along with jewelry and hats.

20″ — #2170. 1957. Cissy in a beautiful bridal gown of nylon tulle with a double train of white satin falling gracefully to the floor. Her veil, which is chapel length, is attached to a coronet of flowers. The bodice of her satin gown is beautifully trimmed with imported satin applique. She wears long white gloves and carries a bridal bouquet. Her jewels are pearl necklace, a solitaire ring, and pearl earrings.

20″ — #2171. 1957. Cissy Queen dressed in a gold brocade court gown. Her gold tiara and earrings sparkle with gems, and she wears a pearl necklace. The blue sash of the garter features the Garter Star. She wears long, white gloves, stockings, and gold sandals. Courtesy Roberta Lago

21″ Princess Grace. (Cissy). 1957. This doll sold for $125.00 in 1957 and is exceptionally gowned. There is gold thread filagree and she wears gold lamé half bodice and sleeves, as well as gloves. This is a special crown. Grace Kelly became Princess Grace in a Royal wedding to Prince Rainier of Monaco on June 19, 1956. This doll was released late in the Fall 1956 and Spring 1957. Hairdo on company brochures is more elaborate than this doll's. Courtesy Connie Bean.

20″ — #2172. 1957. Beautiful, red-headed Cissy dressed for the opera in a blue heavy faille lace-print dress. A wide sweeping circular skirt, fully lined, is worn over beautiful lingerie. Her cape-stole of orlon ermine is satin lined, and her velvet sash is caught at waistline with a garland of roses. She wears a bracelet, pearl earrings and necklace and a shining ring.

20″ —. # 2173. 1957. Red-headed Cissy models her black, velvet gown cut on princess lines. Her cape-stole of natural fur is fastened with a corsage of sweetheart roses (missing in photo). Cissy wears a pearl necklace and earrings and a rhinestone bracelet, long black gloves, crinoline slip, panties and high-heeled sandals.

20″ — #2174. 1957. Sophisticated Cissy in gown of purple velvet with long tight-fitting torso, flaring out at the knee with a flounce of layers and layers of lilac nylon tulle. The off-shoulder gown is lined in the deep decolletage with pink satin, and a rhinestone clip in center of bodice neckline. A large bunch of roses at skirtline, earrings, and bracelet complete her ensemble.

20" — #2175. 1957. Lady Hamilton. Her beautiful floor-length gown is fashioned of blue silk pongee matching her blue eyes. The tight-fitted bodice features a deep neckline. Her shoulder shrug goes over her shoulders and is sewn in the back seam above the waistline. Her silk slip features a hoop sewn above a 6" lace ruffle. A lone large wild rose adorns the front of her stole and matches the roses on her large, natural straw, picture hat. She wears silver high-heeled sandals, pearl earrings and a diamond ring on her finger.

20″ — #2130. 1957. Cissy and her companion, Cissette, are wearing a dress of medium blue polished cotton with lace trim. Large matching picture hat with a single large rose for trim, pearl earrings with gold sets, and a ring completes her ensemble.

20″ — #2110. 1957. Cissy wearing a red taffeta dress with sleeves of red and white polka dot, a large bow giving it a jumper effect. The cloche-shaped hat of white straw is very flattering. She wears nylon stockings, taffeta panties, and black sandals, and a solitaire ring.

20″ — #2141. 1957. Red-headed Cissy wearing a short afternoon navy taffeta dress with abbreviated cape of white-pleated organdy. Her hat of white lacy straw is trimmed with white flowers. Cissy wears a watch circled with rhinestones, a matching bracelet, pearl drop earrings and white imported French gloves.

20″ — #2120. 1957. Cissy is dressed in a nylon yellow print dress, big straw hat, pearl bracelet, with matching earrings and a cameo pin. A wide belt encircles her waist. She wears stockings and sling-back shoes.

21″ — #2119. 1957. Cissy in street clothes of a white lace-trimmed blouse, black felt bolero and full circular skirt. Cissy chose a tiny pink hat, stocking, shoes and a ring as accessories.

21″ — #2146. 1957. Cissy is wearing a short evening dress of navy blue taffeta with tiny cap sleeve. Over her shoulder she wears a white organdy stole trimmed with pink rosebuds. Her tiny tulle and nylon net hat is trimmed with flowers.

21″ Cissy is in a white blouse with ruffles at neck and sleeve edge. She wears a pair of red velvet slacks and around her waist she wears a gold brocade cummerbund-type sash. She wears a bracelet, red sandals and stockings, and roses trim the neckline of the blouse. Sold extra. 1957.

21″ Cissy in a night gown of rayon satin with val lace trim at hem and neckline. Tiny rosebuds of pink with green leaves trim the bodice, and it is tied with a pink satin ribbon. The negligee is a sheer organdy print of light green trimmed with lace at sleeve edge and neck. At her waist she wears a pink satin ribbon. A pair of mules on her feet. This negligee and gown was sold exclusively through F.A.O. Schwarz Co. in 1957. Called "Cissy Takes a Trip", the doll and extra outfits were sold in a trunk.

21″ — #2143. 1957. Cissy wearing a lilac afternoon gown of taffeta with a removable short-sleeved bolero and a flower-trimmed hat to match. She is wearing a bracelet, a ring, pearl earrings, and necklace and is carrying a handbag. She wears a full can-can slip, panties, stockings, and sling-back shoes.

1958 Cissy modeling gowns of classic enchantment that will long be remembered and sought after by collectors.

21″ — #2252. 1958. Beautiful, red-headed Cissy wearing a cocktail dress of pink satin which is ballerina-length. Underneath, her lingerie includes a pink taffeta and net slip, pink, nylon panties, nylon stockings and silver sling-back shoes. In her hair, which is a crown cluster of curls, she wears a small spray of pink roses. Around her neck she wears a string of pearls, matching the pearls encircling an amethyst set in earrings.

21″ — #2280. 1958. Cissy as a bride in a gown of fragile lace lavishly embroidered in a bridal wreath pattern. A full-length veil of tulle attached to a coronet of flowers and a matching bridal bouquet. Her jewelry includes a pearl necklace, earrings and bracelet, and on her finger she wears a solitaire ring.

21″ — #2281. 1958. Queen wearing a court gown of gold brocade, a golden tiara with gems, long, white gloves and glittering jewels; our gracious Queen is truly regal and romantic.

21″ — #2282. 1958. Cissy will long be remembered in her fragile and flowery full-skirted gown. Her beautiful straw picture hat is trimmed with red roses. She wears long white gloves, a pearl necklace and bracelet and a solitaire ring. A very rare doll. Courtesy of Marjorie Biggs.

21″ — #2285. 1958. Beautifully blonde Cissy looks even more lovely in her hollyberry red taffeta with a skirt sweeping to the floor. Her lovely hair arrangement, which is very unusual, with crown curls and 3 rolls of pincurls cascading down back of head and a cluster of curls at neckline. Her sheer froth swiss-dotted, tulle stole covering her hair, drapes over her shoulders and falls to the hem of her long gown. Her jewelry consists of a sparkling ring, and a pearl necklace. A very rare doll. Courtesy of Marjorie Biggs.

21″ — #2283. 1958. Sable brown-haired Cissy is wearing a ball gown of silk, with pink camellias in a wide-spaced print. Her long cape stole, caressing her shoulders, is of velvet, lined to match her gown. Her jewels are a rhinestone cluster pin at bodice neckline, and her neck is encircled with a rhinestone necklace matching the solitaire rhinestone earrings and ring. Her gold veil is caught at the crown with a small spray of flowers. Her under garments consist of nylon panties, silk stockings, and red sandals, and a full-hoop skirt.

21" — #2211. Cissy wearing polka dot dress of polished cotton with a contrasting dotted swiss tulle tie fastened at the crown of her straw hat and tying under her chin. Her navy-blue sandals match her dress. She has beautiful red hair, wears a full cancan slip, panties, nylon stockings and a ring. 1958

21" — #2212. Red-headed Cissy wearing a black jersey blouse with a red print cotton skirt and a gold contour belt. She wears a cancan slip, nylon panties, nylon stockings, black sandals and a solitaire ring. 1958.

21" Cissy is wearing a shirtwaist dress of silk taffeta trimmed with rhinestones and val lace. The bright pink roses in her tiny hat pick up the color of her dress. She wears a black veil. Her undergarments are a nylon print slip with scalloped edges, pink, taffeta panties, and sandals with two ruby sets, and a ring. #22-C18. 1958. Sold extra.

21″ — #2222. 1958. Our blonde, blue-eyed Cissy looks cool in her blue print on white cotton dress. She wears a double-stringed necklace and matching bracelet and earrings. Her large hat is trimmed with white field flowers and her blue sling-back shoes are trimmed with two rhinestones.

21″ — #2230. 1958. Cissy wearing a pink shirtwaist dress with rhinestone buttons and tiny ruffles of lace. A rhinestone trims the points of the cuffs. She has a charming hat trimmed with rosebuds. Her nylon dress is patterned with velour flowers. She wears a slip in velour pattern, gold sandals, silk stockings, a solitaire ring and rhinestone earrings.

21″ — #2214. Cissy wearing a bright-lavender dress of sheer organdy, with a bright-yellow bow and sash. A natural straw hat trimmed with tiny violets adorns her head. She wears taffeta panties, cancan slip, nylon stockings and sandals, and a ring. 1958.

21″ — #2242. Cissy is wearing a flowered print of blue trimmed with white lace and a light-blue straw hat with a large rose. She wears sandals, stockings and a solitaire ring. 1958.

21″ — #2170. 1959. Having a wedding? Why not! Here is Cissy. wearing a full-skirted gown of nylon tulle cascading to the floor over two underskirts. Her fitted bodice and puffed sleeves are trimmed with fine lace. Around her waist is a wide, satin belt tied in a bow in the back with streamers to the floor. Her lovely hairdo of a simple pageboy and bangs is topped by a circle of flowers holding her floor-length veil. She wears a double string of pearls around her neck matching her pearl earrings. 1959 marked the first year a few Cissys were given the graceful, long one-piece arms later to be used on the Jacqueline dolls and Portraits.

21″ — #2118. Cissy wearing a pink taffeta dress, a fur hat, a white taffeta coat with a lilac and lavender ribbon which matches her lilac sandals. She wears a cancan petticoat, a solitaire ring and rhinestone earrings. She has a lovely bisque quality face. 1959. Courtesy Marjorie Biggs.

21″ — #22-60. 1959. Cissy dressed for an evening of fun and dancing in her bright-red organdy dress overlayed with nylon tulle dotted swiss. Her shoulders are covered with an attached stole of matching material. Her hair is elaborate with tiny curls. She wears rhinestone earrings and two, white wild roses at her waist, and a ring. Her under-garments are a black strapless, all-lace chemise, a bright-red taffeta underslip with matching nylon tulle ruffle at the hemline, nylon stockings and red sandals.

21″ — #2150. 1959. Cissy wearing a green satin brocade sleeveless dress. The bodice has tiny gathers at the bust-line, and the skirt is full with unpressed pleats. On her shoulders she wears a matching stole fastened at waist with a gold pin set with rhinestones and emeralds. She wears a gold bracelet with four tiny emerald stones, earrings and a diamond ring. She wears a full nylon slip with scalloped edge trimmed with an under-ruffle of net, elaborate lace-trimmed panties, nylon stockings, green sandals, and a tiny hat of net and tulle trimmed with a garland of pink roses.

21″ Cissy dressed in yellow nylon organdy with an overskirt of matching tulle. Her dress features a cummerbund at waistline trimmed with tiny white flowers and matching flowers on the shoulder. She wears yellow taffeta panties, a yellow taffeta slip with matching tulle ruffle at the hemline, nylons, and gold sandals. Around her neck she wears a gold necklace with pearls, double-drop pearl earrings and a ring. (A tag on her slip reads CD. Company #1324) As her companion she has a tiny sister, Cissette, dressed in an identical outfit.

21" — #2311. Cissy wearing a sleeveless, red and white polka dot dress with a neckline ruffle and a red satin belt. On her head she wears a tiny, red straw hat with white flower trim. She wears panties, stockings and sling-back shoes. 1960.

21" — #2310. Cissy wearing a yellow organdy dress with white flower print, and a yellow ribbon sash. She has rhinestones and lace trimming the bodice of the dress. She wears pearl earrings, a bracelet, and white pumps. Her hat is a fashionable cloche. 1960.

21″ Cissy Scarlett, 1961, as Scarlett O'Hara — #2240. An unforgettable doll from an unforgettable movie, "Gone With the Wind", wearing a blue taffeta gown with black-braid trim matching coat and bonnet, worn over a billowing crinoline petticoat. She wears lace mitts, a cameo necklace, rhinestone earrings, and has a pendent watch pinned to her jacket at the waist. She carries a black lace handbag. This doll is all hard plastic with one-piece arms.

21″ — #2245. 1961. Lissy (Cissy) wearing a mauve pink organdy dress with matching accordian-pleated tulle. Two hundred and ten inches around the bottom of her gown, made with three tiers. She wears square drop earrings with twelve small rhinestones bordering one large rhinestone in center, a rhinestone bracelet, a solitaire ring, and each tier of her gown is trimmed with scallops of sequins matching the sequins on the edge and neckline of her gown. Her undergarments consist of a beautiful taffeta full hoop slip with a six-inch tulle ruffle trimming the hemline, pink taffeta panties, stockings and silver sandals. A spray of flowers at her waist and a high, elaborately braided hairdo. A rare doll

21" Renoir — 1961 — #2250. (Cissy). Renoir is wearing a yellow satin gown with matching jacket, trimmed with black sequins, and she carries a handbag (jeweled) with black sequins. She wears a full net petticoat, white taffeta panties and black sandals. Her headpiece is made of roses, violets, and field flowers and is attached to a black veil. Her jewelry consists of cameo earrings and necklace, and a diamond ring. She is all hard plastic with long, graceful one-piece arms.

21″ Godey of 1961. Uses the Cissy face with walker body and one piece vinyl arms. Soft, lavender satin gown with deeper lavender-purple velvet coat jacket. Courtesy Pat Smith.

21" — #2235. Melanie. A "Gone With The Wind" Portrait doll. Deep blue slipper satin gown with over dress of lace. Elaborate hairdo in the style of the Godey era.

Lace coat is replacement. 1961. (Courtesy Charmaine Shields.)

21" — #2170. 1962. Bride. Cissy bride elaborately dressed in beige lace over white-pleated tulle. Her dress features bracelet-length sleeves, a scalloped hemline. Her veil cascades to the floor and is held in place by a crown of flowers. She wears a full crinoline petticoat, nylon panties, stockings and silver slippers. She wears a pearl bracelet, necklace and earrings, a solitaire ring and carries her traditional bridal bouquet.

21″ Godey. #2260. 1962. (Cissy) Godey, wearing a white and bright-orange gown. The bodice is of white organdy, trimmed with lace and rhinestone buttons. Her jacket is of matching velvet and is trimmed at the sleeve edge with white lace matching ruffles on the bodice. She is wearing a natural straw hat with large pink roses and field flowers that are covered with a pink veil pulled to the back of her hat and tied with a bow and cascading streamers. She wears rhinestone earrings, and on her wrist dangles a pendant of amethyst and rhinestones, and she wears an amethyst ring on her finger.

21" Queen Elizabeth II of England (Cissy), 1962, #2180. Our Queen faces her court in a gown of gold brocade decorated with the sash of the Order of the Bath. She wears rhinestone earrings, two rhinestone bracelets on one wrist and a solitaire ring. Her gold crown has three large stones. She wears a long crinoline slip, taffeta panties and gold slippers. A fully-jointed plastic doll, jointed even at her knees, she has one-piece, long, graceful arms.

Each year the Ice Capades Design and Costume Dept. dress a doll for each of the production numbers using the Skating Ice Capettes. By doing this they discover any errors that may happen, can judge the use of materials and can also "see" the finished costume. This saves the company a large amount of money over the years. The dolls are then used by the lighting and staging departments to help create the effects that they want.

The dolls are the result of a great amount of work and each little detail is important. The dolls are insured to $500.00 each and many have been sent on the road for department store displays, as well as television publicity appearances. They are returned to the Ice Capades home office and put on display.

A few years ago Ice Capades disposed of some of these one of a kind dolls, and they are beginning to find their way into private collections.

The design department did not pay any attention to the doll, as long as it had a fairly-adult appearance, they used it. Some of these dolls are composition, Kaysam dolls of 1961, Alexanders and there are even some Italian dolls included.

During the late 1950's and early 1960's, Ice Capades used Alexander dolls (Cissy) and then later after 1965, they used the Jacqueline-faced doll for a few of their production dolls.

This Ice Capades doll is a Cissy and used in 1961-1962 in the "My Fair Lady" number. One-piece vinyl arms and the hard plastic knee joints have been glued in place within the tight skirt. The wigs on the dolls with head pieces have been removed by the designers at Ice Capades, and each doll (Ice Capette) is fitted with a tight "wig" head piece. Courtesy Pat Smith.

21″ Ice Capades doll from the number "Showboat". 1963. Standard Cissy doll of 1960's with the one piece vinyl arms. Courtesy Pat Smith.

This is a flat-footed Cissy-faced Binnie Walker that was used for an Indian from the "Adventurers of Peter Pan" number of 1956 and her name is "Tiger Lily". Courtesy Pat Smith.

21″ Cissy used by the Ice Capades for the production number Cole Porter of 1963.

Elise, 16½″ tall, 1957 first year. Made of hard plastic with jointed vinyl arms and jointed ankles. She can wear either high or low heeled shoes.

Elise, #1638, 1957. A beautiful bridesmaid dressed in a gown of organdy with an overlay of dotted nylon net. Around her waist she wears a pink satin bow picking up the color of her gown. Underneath she wears a full taffeta slip with nylon tulle ruffle at the hemline, silk hose, a matching pearl necklace and bracelet and silver shoes. (Minus her basket of flowers. Matte Finish on face.)

Elise, #1610, 1957, 16½″ tall. Elise modeling a pink checked taffeta dress with white organdy sleeves and Peter Pan collar. She wears a white straw hat with pink field flowers as trim. She wears a white lace slip scalloped at the hemline, white taffeta panties, stockings, and pink sandals.

Elise, #1632, 1957. Elise goes shopping in a popular jumper style dress of cocoa brown. Her blouse is a soft pink crepe with bow at neckline. She wears a cocoa brown hat and a golden charm bracelet.

Elise is all hard plastic, jointed elbows, knees and ankles. Elise wearing a red-polished afternoon dress with white cuffs and buttons on bodice for trim. She wears a fashionable hat with a red ribbon around the crown and streamers.

Elise, #1750, 1958, 16½″ tall. A beautiful bride in a traditional gown of sheer tulle embroidered in bridal-
wreath design, a tulle veil falling to the floor and attached to a coronet of flowers. Her shoulders are covered
with an attached stole. She wears a full taffeta underslip, taffeta panties, the traditional bridal garter, nylons
and silver slippers. A pearl necklace, bracelet, and earrings.

Elise, #1835, 1959, 16½″ tall. Elise dressed in a very unusual bridal gown of pale pink nylon tulle. She has large, puffed sleeves trimmed with lace of pink and matching the lace down the bodice of her gown. She wears a long, pink veil of tulle and a coronet of flowers matching her bridal bouquet. She wears pearl earrings and a ring.

There was also a Cissette made, dressed in this same outfit. Gown identical to Cissy Bride 1959.

Elise, #1815, 1959. Elise goes to play bridge with the girls dressed in a sheer nylon sprinkled with pastel flowers. She wears a darling pink hat of straw with blossoms and a pink veil. A velvet ribbon sash at her waistline, pearl necklace, earrings and a ring. Nylon taffeta slip, panties, stockings and gold sandals.

Elise Ballerina, #1810, 1959. Graceful Elise dressed in a tutu of layers and layers of gold net. Her bodice of gold cloth has a deep yoke trimmed with matching sequins. She has a gold tiara and matching ballet slippers and tiny gold earrings.

#1735, 1960 Elise. Our beautiful bride is dressed in a gown of white satin with long, satin streamers cascading to the floor in back. The simple bodice has a wide lace bertha trimmed with sequins and crystal beads and has bracelet length sleeves. On her head she wears a coronet of flowers attached to a floor-length veil of tulle. She is carrying a bridal bouquet and is wearing a necklace of pearls, matching earrings and an engagement ring. Courtesy Millie Ferguson.

Approximate year, 1963, Elise, hard plastic, jointed arms, legs, and ankles. Elise in a mauve pink, all dressed for a wedding dance in her gown of nylon tulle with a full skirt of unpressed pleats and self-ruffles around the sleeves. Long white gloves, rhinestone earrings, and a rhinestone bracelet. Elise chose to carry her pink straw hat so as to show off her newly-styled short hair.

Elise, #1750, 1962, and her little sister, #755, Cissette. A spun sugar confection of nylon tulle and lace. Her beautiful coronet is attached to her floor-length veil. She wears a pearl necklace, pearl earrings, and a solitaire ring. Her undergarments are two petticoats — one of organdy and one of tulle. She wears nylon lace panties, stockings, silver sandals and carries a bridal bouquet of tiny, pink and white flowers. (Marybel face) Elise of this year was 17 inches tall.

#1740. 1962. Elise in her blue tutu with bodice of sequins to match her coronet. She has blonde hair, blue eyes and wears pink pantyhose and pink ballet slippers. She wears tiny rhinestone earrings. This particular Elise has a vinyl face, jointed ankles, knees and elbows.

Elise, 1962, dressed in a cotton-checked dress of teal blue and made shirtwaist style. Her three-quarter length sleeve is trimmed with a white cuff and matched the little white collar at the neckline. Two rows of lace on either side of the button closure trim the bodice. She wears a matching coat and hat of blue with rosebuds at the neckline. She wears a can-can slip, panties, nylon stockings and high-heeled sandals. She wears a blue, grosgrain ribbon sash, and tiny pearl earrings. Her unusual hat is trimmed with flowers and feathers. All hard plastic.

18" Elise #1765, 1963. Renoir, as pretty as a painting. Her gown is of mauve pink taffeta with five rows of val lace down front of bodice. Circling her waist is black braid, matching braid on the edge of her three-quarter length sleeves. Her pink taffeta reticule is trimmed with a wide band of black lace. Around her neck she wears a cameo hanging from a black velvet ribbon matching the tiny black velvet bows on the ruffle of her dress. She wears three-stone rhinestone earrings, a solitaire ring and a beautiful flowered hat tied under her chin with a pink veil. She wears a white crinoline petticoat with a wide net ruffle on the inside, white taffeta panties and black shoes.

18" Scarlett, #1760, 1963. Elise dressed as the famous southern belle, Scarlett O'Hara. Her dress is pale blue organdy trimmed with lace tucks, and rosebuds worn over a pale blue organdy underlay. Around her waist she wears a satin sash with long streamers to the hem of her dress. The neckline is trimmed with a wide ruffle and her sleeves have an unusual design with a full puff from above and ending just below the elbow. Her waistline and her skirt are trimmed with rosebuds matching the flowers on her picture hat of straw. She wears gold filigree earrings and a solitaire ring. She wears a crinoline slip, long white lace-trimmed pantaloons, stockings and silver slippers. This doll has a Marybel face. Rare Doll.

18″ Elise, #1780, 1963. Queen Elizabeth II of England looking as a Queen should in a ball gown of white brocade decorated with a sash of the Order of the Bath. She wears rhinestone earrings, a twin-stone diamond ring, a rhinestone and ruby bracelet, long white gloves and a jeweled tiara, with a large cluster of jewels in the center. She wears a long crinoline petticoat, stockings, panties, and gold slippers. Only year Elise was used as a queen. The Queen, Scarlett, and Renior were made with both a hard plastic and a Marybel face.

18″ Elise Ballerina. #1720. 1963. Elise in a blue pleated tutu with nylon tights and ballet slippers of pink satin. Tiny roses sprinkled over her tutu and a wreath of flowers in her hair. A blue satin ribbon fastened at the waist and tying in back in a bow. She wears tiny rhinestone earrings. She has a Marybel face, jointed ankles, knees and elbows.

18″ Elise bride, 1964, #1740. Elise's gown is made of tiers of beautiful lace with lace bodice and puffed sleeves. Her coronet of orange blossoms attached to a chapel-length veil. White satin bow at waistline, a pearl necklace, a sparkling ring and a bridal bouquet of pale spring flowers. She wears the traditional garter. She is jointed at elbows, knees and ankles. Her companion is Wendy #630, 1965.

Elise, going to prom, approximately 1964. She wears an organdy gown of lilac with tiers of lace from hipline to floor. The bodice of her gown is trimmed with matching lace and around her waist, she wears a satin sash tied in a bow in the back. In her hair she wears tiny rosebuds that match the flowers on her skirt. She wears double-drop pearl earrings and necklace.

Elise, 1964, dressed as a beautiful debutante in a pale blue gown with a full skirt trimmed with 19 rows of lace. Her dress features a square neckline trimmed with lace and showing off her pretty pearl necklace and double-drop earrings. She wears long, white gloves, a pale blue slip with matching panties, silver sandals. In her hair she wears a rose matching the roses on her skirt. Elise is hard plastic with vinyl face and arms. She is jointed at the ankles, knees, and elbows. (Courtesy Marge Meisinger)

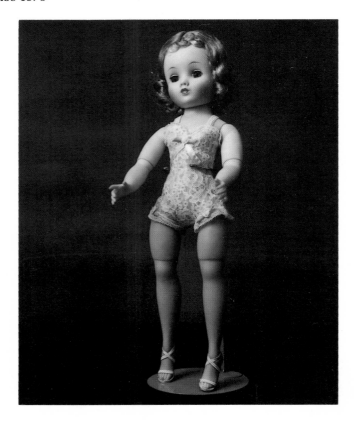

16½ — Basic Elise in Chemise. Jointed at arms and knees and ankles. She is all hard plastic except arms. They are vinyl. Drop pearl earrings. Lace Chemise has pink ribbon and ribbon flowers at breast and at legs. Courtesy — Roberta Lago.

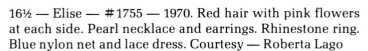

16½ — Elise — #1755 — 1970. Red hair with pink flowers at each side. Pearl necklace and earrings. Rhinestone ring. Blue nylon net and lace dress. Courtesy — Roberta Lago

16½ — Elise Bride. Rhinestone ring, pearl necklace, pearl earrings, and pearls on bridal cap. Dress is nylon net with satin ribbon at waist and tying in back. Replaced bouquet. Blond with blue eyes. White satin pumps. Courtesy — Roberta Lago

Elise bride, 1970, #1765. Our bride is a picture to behold in her tulle and lace gown with long sleeves, lace-trimmed bodice. The hemline and down the center of her gown is trimmed with lace. Atop her beautifully styled hair she wears a floral tiara holding her veil. She is wearing pearl earrings and necklace and a ring on her finger, satin shoes and long stockings. She is posed ready to throw her bridal bouquet to the next lucky girl.

17" Elise ballerina, #1715, 1971. Elise dressed in a pink satin and tulle rosebud trimmed ballet dress. In her hair she wears a floral tiara. She wears a black velvet band at her throat, pink satin ballet slippers, nylon pantyhose, and pearl earrings.

Portrait Elise, #1780, 1972. Elise wears a full-skirted nylon dress with a pleated ruffle at the hemline, rosebud trimmed, ruffled neckline, and puffed sleeves. She wears a sparkling brooch, a sash at her waist tied in a bow, and a ring on her finger. A pink straw hat with lace edging and trimmed with flowers and a satin ribbon. Her straight, long, blonde hair falls to her waistline. She wears a full crinoline slip, pink nylon panties, stockings and pink, satin shoes.

Elise, #1750, 1972. Elise in tulle and lace with a black velvet ribbon around her neck, tiny rhinestone earrings, and a cluster of flowers and ribbon in her hair. She wears matching sandals, taffeta panties, and a wide-ribbon sash.

#2210, 1961 Jacqueline 21″ in a beautiful strapless gown of white satin with matching full-length capecoat. She has soft, brown eyes and brunette hair parted on the left side with a wisp of a curl in the center. White taffeta panties, stockings and sling-back shoes complete her attire. She wears a diamond ring, a bracelet, pearl necklace, and a pearl frog catches her coat at the neckline. Dress is basic pattern of Princess style used throughout portraits.

Mimi — 1961 — 21". Made from Jacqueline mold. Our brown-eyed brunette's hair is pulled into a bun of curls at the back of her head with shorter hair on each side and bangs in front. Her two-piece ensemble is tagged inside, Halin's Doll Fashions, Chicago. The collarless dress and jacket are made of gold metallic material. Four self-covered buttons go down the front of the jacket. She wears white taffeta panties, silk stockings and gold sling-back shoes. She carries a small brocade purse and wears a diamond ring on her finger. There are other collectors who have small dolls dressed with the same name on the tag. Sold through Wanamakers, Vincents (K.C.) and Neiman-Marcus (Dallas) — 1961.

Jacqueline — #2133 — 1961 — 21". Jacqueline dressed in a four-piece outfit. Her bright-orange jersey blouse goes well with her emerald-green corduroy slacks and matching corduroy hat. She is warmly dressed if the day is chilly in her beige vinyl jacket. She wears green sandals and a sparkling ring. This outfit was bought in a box.

21" "Embassy Tea". Jacqueline wearing a pink gown of heavy slipper satin. To cover her shoulders she wears a lace jacket trimmed with rhinestones. The neck of the jacket is trimmed with pearl beading. Under her lovely gown she wears a stiff crinoline slip, and pink taffeta panties. This gown was to be sold during 1962-63 as a boxed outfit but was not as doll was discontinued.

21″ — #2130, 1962. Jacqueline is pictured on the cover of the 1962 Alexander catalog. Jacqueline is looking beautiful indeed in a strapless, silver and white brocade evening gown with matching short jacket caught at the waistline with a pearl-trimmed hook. She wears a cri- noline slip, white taffeta panties, stockings and silver sling-back shoes. She also wears pearl and rhinestone earrings, a pearl necklace and a sparkling ring on her finger.

21″ — #2135 — 1962. Jacqueline is wearing a stunning ball gown of brocade with flaring panels of red satin. Pearl necklace, bracelet, and a ring are her choice for this ensemble. Courtesy Charmaine Shields.

21″ — #2117. 1962. Jacqueline all ready to take a horse-back ride with Caroline. Mother and daughter wear matching outfits. Caroline #1312 — 15″.

17″ Maggie Mix-Up, #1855. Maggie Mix-Up and companion, little Maggie Mix-Up. Maggie dressed for an afternoon in town in a skirt and blouse worn over leotards and a taffeta petticoat. Her skirt is hot pink trimmed with striped ribbon and rickrack. Atop her head she wears a bright-pink hat with flowers, around her neck is a golden heart necklace.

21″ Piper Laurie. All hard plastic. 1950. Flat feet. Flaming red hair. Silk organza gown. Margaret face. Courtesy Memory Brengle.

16½″ Maggie Mix-Up, #1812, 1960. Maggie dressed in a lace-trimmed, white cotton blouse and a checked jumper. A straw hat on top of her red-gold hair is trimmed with a blue ribbon. Freckles on her cute little nose give her an air of mischievousness. She wears Capezio-type slippers and long black tights, a golden necklace with golden heart, and a lace-trimmed slip.

Maggie Mix-Up was made two years only, 1960 and 1961. Her body construction is of light plastic and her arms are vinyl. She is made with an Elise body, with jointed ankles and knees.

16½″ Maggie Mix-Up, #1811, 1960. Dressed for a day of fun, of bicycling or perhaps a picnic, whichever pleases her fancy, in long-tailored slacks with white jersey blouse and a striped sash. She wears a golden necklace, straw hat, and gold slippers. Courtesy Mariam Knox.

16½″ Maggie Mix-Up in outfit sold separately from doll, 1961. Maggie wearing a one-piece of polka dot and pink creating a jumper effect. She wears a straw hat trimmed in pink and flat slippers. Dress tag reads "Madame Alexander." Courtesy Korina Kay Macgurn.

17″ Maggie Mix-Up, #1850, 1961. Maggie models a cardigan and long dress slacks with pockets and a fun hat with a bee, a bell and a little bird with a crazy lavender hat, flat slippers with a tiny red ball on the toe of her shoe. She has red-gold hair, green eyes and freckles on her nose.

17″ Maggie Mix-Up, #1855. Maggie models the same outfit in blue with yellow, red, and blue poppies on her hat. Her tights are a violet blue matching the ribbon in her skirt and with it she wears beige flats with gold trim. Around her neck dangles a gold sweetheart locket.

17″ Polly, #1751. (Dress tag reads she sold for $14.95.) Permanent-pleated bouffant skirt, mauve pink tulle formal with matching pink sequined bodice tells us Polly is all ready for an evening of fun. She wears stockings, satin slippers of matching velvet and a ring on her finger. Her long, red hair is entwined with sequins.

17″ Polly, #1724. 1965, made one year only. A glamorous young lady, Polly, is dressed in white cotton lace with a pale-blue lining, taffeta panties, and a blue taffeta slip. Wearing stockings, flat slippers and a tiny bow in her long, blonde hair styled in an unusual way with tiny curls at the crown. She wears a cluster of flowers at her waist, a ring on her finger and in sharp contrast to her blonde hair she has black eyes. (Pupil less)

17″ — #1715. Polly dressed in an apricot-striped dress with matching polka dot, ruffled trim. She wears slip, panties, long stockings and shoes and wears a ring on her finger.

17″ Polly, dress tagged "Madame Alexander". Polly is wearing a white cotton dress with red ribbon trim at hemline and down center of dress. A red ribbon bow at the neckline matches the bows in her long brunette hair.

17″ — 1965, Leslie, black doll. Leslie and Polly are made from the same mold. Leslie, #1620, in a charming pink and white cotton dress. The hemline is trimmed with lace, and around her shoulders is a lace shawl. She wears a lace-trimmed cotton slip with matching panties and pink suede shoes. Her dress is tagged, "Madame Alexander, All rights reserved." Her wrist tag reads "Leslie".

17" Mary Ellen playmate, exclusively made and dressed for Marshall Field Company in 1965. Her dress tag reads, "Mary Ellen Playmate (Polly)." (Courtesy Marge Meisinger)

A Family Portrait

*Front row*
*Left to right*

Godey — 1969
Southern Belle — 1970
Scarlett — 1968 — (first year)
Southern Belle — 1968
Melinda — 1968
Melanie — 1969

*2nd row*
*Left to right*

Jacqueline — 1962
Melanie — 1970
Renoir — 1968 — (red hat)
Godey — 1968
Agatha — 1968
Jenny Lind — 1969
Southern Belle — 1970

*3rd row*
*Left to right*

Southern Belle — 1967
Gold Rush — 1963
Margot — *(kneeling)*
Renoir — 1969
Queen — 1972 or 1973
Jenny Lind — 1970

# PORTRAITS
## 1965-1978

The year 1965 saw the introduction of the Portrait Series using the Jacqueline doll of 1961-1962. All the Portraits, either 1965 or year 1978, have the same mold information. They will all be dated 1961 on the back of the necks.

All Portraits have blue eye shadow and dresses tagged with the name of the doll with the exception of 1965 and 1966 dolls. The 1965 and 1966 tags read: "Madame Alexander." All rights reserved, New York, U.S.A. 1966 is also an exception in that the CoCo doll was used for the Portraits rather than the Jacqueline doll.

The following is a complete listing of all the Portrait dolls to date. (1978). The #2295 — 1976 Scarlett and the #2296 — 1977 Scarlett are identical to the Scarlett of 1975, therefore the 1975 one will be shown only:

**1965**
#2151 — Bride
#2152 — Scarlett
#2155 — Southern Belle
#2154 — Renoir
#2153 — Godey
#2150 — Queen

**1966** (CoCo)
#2060 — Madame Doll
#2063 — Godey
#2050 — Melanie
#2061 — Scarlett
#2051 — Lissy
#2062 — Renoir

**1967**

#2174 — Scarlett
#2175 — Renoir
#2170 — Southern Belle
#2172 — Godey
#2173 — Melanie
#2171 — Agatha

**1968**
#2182 — Lady Hamilton
#2181 — Melanie
#2180 — Scarlett
#2184 — Gainsborough
#2183 — Goya
#2185 — Queen

**1969**
#2193 — Melanie
#2195 — Godey
#2192 — Bride
#2191 — Jenny Lind
#2190 — Scarlett
#2194 — Renoir

**1970**
#2181 — Jenny Lind
#2184 — Renoir
#2196 — Melanie
#2195 — Godey
#2197 — Madame Pompadour
#2180 — Scarlett

**1971**
#2170 — Mimi
#2163 — Renoir
#2162 — Melanie
#2161 — Godey

**1972**
#2191 — Cornelia
#2190 — Renoir
#2192 — Gainsborough

**1973**
#2190 — Renoir
#2191 — Cornelia
#2192 — Gainsborough

**1974**
#2296 — Cornelia
#2295 — Melanie
#2294 — Agatha

**1975**
#2291 — Agatha
#2292 — Scarlett
#2290 — Cornelia

**1976**
#2293 — Cornelia
#2294 — Agatha
#2295 — Scarlett

**1977**
#2297 — Magnolia
#2298 — Godey
#2296 — Scarlett

**1978**
#2212 — Cornelia
#2210 — Scarlett
#2211 — Gainsborough

21" Southern Belle. 1965. #2155. The picture can never do her justice. A true Southern belle wearing a pale-blue dress of nylon tulle. Bodice has lace in a v from waist to shoulder, with tiny beads around the pattern of the lace. A deep flounce of finely-pleated tulle borders the skirt and matches the pleating around the neckline. The dress is underlaid with additional attached tulle and organdy slips. She has matching short taffeta pant-ies, stockings and silver sling-back shoes. The blonde, blue-eyed Southern belle has an elaborate hairdo. Tiny curls crown the top of the head with rolls of curls to the neckline. Three sequined swags come over the front of the hairdo. Tiny pink rosebuds decorate the skirt and the waistline. She wears two blue rhinestone bracelets and a diamond ring.

21″ Scarlett, 1965, #2152 is a very rare doll. Her dress is of emerald green satin with three-quarter length sleeves and v-neckline trimmed in white lace with black velvet interlacing. She is blue-eyed with dark brunette hair. Scarlett is wearing a white slip and panties, stockings and black sling-back shoes. Her large hat of natural straw is trimmed with green velvet ribbon and flowers, and she is wearing a rhinestone bracelet and a diamond ring.

21″ Portrait 1965 Queen. The gown is rose gold brocade, the crown is silver and has three rhinestones. The front hair is pulled up to the top and is surrounded by the crown. She wears blue stone bracelets and a rhinestone solitaire.

21" 1965 Bride #2151 has pupil-less black eyes and is a brunette. She wears a white satin gown, lace overskirt with a scalloped edge decorated with scattered sequins, over a pleated tulle underskirt. Neck and waistline are decorated with three rows of white sequins. She has drop pearl earrings with gold filigree, a pearl necklace and a diamond ring. Her floor-length veil is trimmed with wide lace matching her skirt and is attached to a crown of flowers. Her hair is double swagged with a cluster of pin curls at the crown. She has a crinoline slip, taffeta panties and silver sling-back shoes.

Renoir, 1965, #2154 has sleeveless taffeta dress with pleated trim and two rows of lace from neck to waist of bodice. Three-quarter length sleeves of the jacket are trimmed with crochet. The matching bonnet is trimmed with lace and pink roses. Renoir wears rhinestone earrings, bracelet and a diamond ring on her finger. She has a white, very stiff slip, white taffeta panties, stockings and open sling-back shoes.

Coco Twenty-inch, soft plastic and vinyl, Madame Alexander used an entirely (New) face for the year 1966. This mold was used in 1966 only for Coco dressed in five outfits and for the Portraits of which there were six, Madame Doll, #2060, Melanie, #2050, Lissy, #2051, and Godey #2063, Scarlett, #2061, and Renoir,

#2062. Coco doll dressed in: 1. A slim skirt with a short orange jacket and ties in cotton. 2. A silk printed sheath. 3. Ruffled organdy trims sleeves and neckline of a pin-stripe sheath. 4. A sheath ball gown of pink brocade trimmed with pink marabou. 5. A black and white jersey jumpsuit with yellow satin ankle-length coat.

21″ — 1966, #2061, Coco Scarlett with long brunette hair, brown eyes and is wearing a white tulle dress with deep six inch lace trim and scattered red roses. The lace over tulle bodice has a pearl-beaded neckline and three-quarter length sleeves trimmed in white lace. She has a white horsehair picture hat trimmed with white flowers, rhinestone earrings and a diamond ring. The dress has an attached slip of organdy, white taffeta panties and white satin shoes with red bows. Courtesy of Mrs. (Velma) Gee

21″ — 1966 Lissy, (Coco), #2051, is brown-eyed and red-headed and dressed in a pink, short-sleeved dress. The satin bodice with an overlay of lace extends down to the hipline of the tulle-pleated skirt which has an organdy underlay. She has matching panties, stockings and white satin slippers with white bows. Her jewelry is a rhinestone tiara, circle rhinestone earrings, a bracelet and a diamond ring. Our red-head's hair is pulled up at the neckline and tied in a ponytail effect with waves and ringlets at the ends of the hair.

21″ Madame Doll, #2060, 1966 (CoCo) is a very rare doll, dressed identical to the 14″ Madame doll. The blue-eyed blonde is dressed in a pink silk brocade gown and pink organdy duster cap. The dress is trimmed with two rows of lace down the front of the skirt. It has a lace-trimmed bodice, neckline and three-quarter length sleeves. She has a cotton slip and pantaloons trimmed in lace. Pearl earrings and necklace and a diamond ring are her jewelry. No secret pocket, although the 14″ size dolls have the secret pocket with pearls.

21″ 1966 Coco Melanie #2050 is dressed in pale-blue taffeta, trimmed in beige lace. The lace goes around the neck to a point at the waistline. Two separate rows of lace with elastic are attached to the sleeves approximately two inches apart forming puffs. The front waistline of the skirt has an insert of fine pleats trimmed on each side with two-inch lace. Our blonde beauty has two long braids encircling her head of curls. She has a crinoline slip, white taffeta panties, stockings and blue, satin shoes with rhinestone settings. She wears a cameo necklace and a diamond ring.

21″ — Renoir/CoCo, #2060, 1966 wears a taffeta gown, braid and lace trimmed, with a coat and matching bonnet. The gown is worn over a crinoline petticoat, taffeta panties, stockings and black velvet slippers. Our brown-eyed redhead wears rhinestone drop earrings and a diamond ring.

21″ — 1966 Godey/CoCo, #2063 is wearing a red taffeta, sleeveless dress trimmed with black lace. The black velvet jacket matches her black velvet hat rim- med with black tulle and a beautiful red rose. She wears a full crinoline slip with white taffeta panties. Our blue-eyed blond is also wearing red velvet slippers.

21″ — #2174, Scarlett, Blue eyes and brunette hair, is dressed in emerald-green, taffeta sleeveless gown with matching jacket trimmed with black braid and white lace. A row of white lace trims the sleeve edge of her dress, jacket, and inside of her matching bonnet. She has a full crinoline slip, white cotton pantaloons trimmed in white lace with green ribbon inserts. Stockings, black sling back shoes and a diamond ring complete her ensemble. The 11″ portrette, Scarlett #1174 made in 1968 is her shadow.

21″ — Agatha, 1967, #2171 is a brown-eyed brunette dressed in red velvet, strapless dress cut on princess lines. The matching jacket is trimmed with beige lace. Her hat is made out of a circle of velvet trimmed with scalloped braid and shaped to the head with fine wire and covered with red tulle to frame her face. She has a full, white crinoline slip, white taffeta panties, silk stockings, and red sling-back shoes. Her jewelry consists of rhinestone drop earrings, gold chain and gold pendant with rhinestone set and diamond ring. Her matching shadow is #1171, 11″, 1968 Agatha.

21″ — Renoir, 1967, #2175 has brunette hair and brown eyes. She is wearing a navy-blue, sleeveless dress with matching laee trim on the armholes. The short jacket is trimmed with pleating that matches the deep-pleated flounce on the bottom of the dress. Three-quarter length sleeves of the jacket are edged with white lace. She has a white crinoline slip, white taffeta panties, stockings and white navy blue pumps. Her red taffeta hat is adorned with red field flowers. She wears double-drop earrings and a diamond ring, and is shadowed by portrette #1175, 1968.

21″ — #2173, 1967 Melanie has blue eyes, blonde hair and is dressed in turquoise blue taffeta dress with white silk yoke trimmed in lace. Pleated ruffles around yoke edge match the ruffle in apron fashion on the skirt. White horsehair picture hat is pulled up and rolled back to form a bonnet with blue and white flowers on the crown and a blue nylon net tie under the chin. She has a full, white crinoline slip, silk stockings, white taffeta panties, and blue pumps. 11″ portrette #1173, made in 1968 and called Melinda is her shadow.

21″ — Southern Belle #2170, 1967. Our blonde is dressed in a white taffeta gown with three ruffles, the bottom one is a deep-pleated flounce. Each ruffle is trimmed in white lace with green ribbon inserts as are the three-quarter length sleeves and the v-neckline. She has an attached underskirt of organdy and a full-length slip of crinoline, matching panties, stockings and green taffeta pumps. Her jewelry consists of cameo necklace, double-drop pearl earrings and a diamond ring. She is shadowed by 1968 portrette #1170.

21″ — 1967, #2172, Godey has red hair, blue eyes and is wearing a dress of beige lace over pink taffeta trimmed with a full ruffle at the hemline and a second ruffle in apron fashion. The full-length sleeves have beige lace around edges matching lace around neckline. Her natural straw bonnet is trimmed with pink tulle and pink rosebuds. She has a pink crinoline slip with an inside flounce of net, matching pink panties, stockings and satin slippers. Double-drop pearl earrings and ring complete the ensemble. She is pictured with her shadow, portrette #1172, 1968.

21″ — #2180, 1968 Scarlett has deep-green eyes, long-lashed and brunette hair. Scarlett's dress is cotton with a cream background and a rose print. The deep white organdy flounce is edged at the top with eyelet ribbon that matches the trim on the large v-neck collar. Green velvet ribbon encircles her waist and ties in a bow at back. She carries a green taffeta umbrella trimmed with white lace. Her natural straw picture hat is encircled at the crown with a green velvet ribbon that matches the ribbon that ties under her chin. The skirt of her dress is underlaid with a cotton, attached, lace-trimmed slip. She wears two three-quarter length taffeta slips with deep heavy net flounce, cotton panties, stockings and green velvet shoes. A rhinestone encircled cameo necklace and a diamond ring are her jewelry.

21" — 1968 Lady Hamilton, #2182 has deep blue eyes with extra-long lashes. She is wearing a gown of beige lace over pink taffeta with a square neckline and large, puffed sleeves. This one-piece dress has a deep flounce with scalloped edges sewn in at the waistline and caught up with a garland of flowers at each side. Her picture hat is natural straw trimmed in pink ribbon and flowers to match those on the dress. She has a stiff pink crinoline slip sewn as one over heavy net with an inside 6" ruffle sewn inside the slip. She also has pink taffeta panties, long hose and pink satin slippers. Her jewelry consists of pearl drop earrings with gold filigree, pearl necklace, bracelet and diamond ring.

21" — Melanie, 1968, #2181. Brown-haired, brown-eyed Melanie wears an unusual gown of rust-colored faille. Her dress is cut on princess lines with gathers at the waist in back. Her strapless gown has a very unusual design of rust-brown braid. Her jacket is trimmed with braid and beige lace matching the lace inside of her bonnet. Her bonnet is of rust-brown velvet and matching taffeta. She has a heavy crinoline slip, white taffeta panties, and brown taffeta pumps. Her jewelry is a cameo necklace encircled with rhinestones and a diamond ring. She finishes her ensemble with a purse of heavy velvet matching her hat.

21″ — Gainsborough, 1968, #2184 is an auburn-haired, blue-eyed beauty, wearing a heavy faille, short-sleeved, aqua-blue gown with matching jacket with an overlay of white lace trimmed with heavy matching braid. The skirt of her dress has two deep tucks around the bottom. Her hat is of a matching tulle which ties under her chin in a bow. She has a crinoline slip lined with heavy net, white taffeta panties, long silk stockings, and silver slippers. Her silver drop earrings have a lone rhinestone set, and her pendant watch is encircled with rhinestones. She wears a diamond ring.

21″ — 1968, Queen, #2185 is ash-blonde, blue-eyed and wears a gown of satin brocade with glitter. She wears elbow-length white gloves, and the sash of the Order of the Bath with jewels. She has a full crinoline slip, white taffeta panties, and white taffeta pumps. Her jewelry is a pearl necklace, earrings with seven rhinestones, a five-point tiara, three-jeweled bracelets, one with rubies and two with rhinestones, and a diamond ring. Her shadow is portrette Queen, #1186 made in 1971.

21″ — 1968, Goya, #2183. Our blonde, blue-eyed Goya is an unusual dress of pink taffeta with a full skirt and eight tiers of ruffles. The bodice has two ruffles from the waist over the shoulder giving the effect of a pinafore. The set-in sleeves are of white cotton circled by nine rows of white one-half inch lace matching the lace around the neckline. Her bonnet too is very unusual, made of pink taffeta in a horn shape with elastic at intervals to make puffs. Inside the bonnet is white lace and on the brim are two large pink rosebuds. The bonnet ties under her chin with a pink satin bow. She wears a heavy-lined crinoline with a full ruffle inside, pink taffeta panties, stockings and pink taffeta pumps. Her jewelry consists of a lone diamond ring.

21" — #2191, 1969 Jenny Lind is dressed beautifully in pink satin with deep neckline and full-length sleeves trimmed with white lace. She carries a large bouquet of light pink and pink rosebuds. Her blonde hair is in an unsual style with a part in the middle and a huge puff on each side. She wears a white crinoline, lined with heavy net and long, pink taffeta pantaloons edged in pink lace at the ankles. She also has pink sling-back shoes. Her jewelry is long rhinestone earrings, roses in her hair and a diamond ring. Her shadow is portrette # 1171 made in 1969.

21" — 1969 Bride, #2192 is blonde and blue-eyed. Her dress is white lace-lined with taffeta. The neck and waistline are trimmed with sequins. Her long sleeves are trimmed with white lace matching the white lace on the bottom of the scalloped skirt. She wears an underskirt of pleated nylon tulle. Her veil is floor-length and caught at the crown with a garland of white flowers. Her undergarments consist of an attached crinoline. At the back waist is a satin ribbon bustle approximately 4" wide and falling to the hem of her skirt. She wears long white taffeta pantaloons trimmed at the ankle with white lace and satin ribbon. Her ball-shaped pearl earrings are trimmed with gold filigree and she wears a diamond ring and carries a bouquet of white orange blossoms.

21″ #2195, 1969 Godey, blonde and blue-eyed is dressed in a strapless gown of red velvet cut on princess lines. Her matching seven-eighths length coat is trimmed at sleeve and coat edge with two rows of black braid. Her black straw hat features a black veil covering her face. The inside of the brim is made of red grosgrain ribbon. Her undergarments are a full net-lined crinoline, and white taffeta pantaloons trimmed at the ankles with white lace. She wears red sling-backs. Her drop earrings are a square of rhinestone sets with a ruby center. Her necklace is a large, oblong ruby. She wears short, black gloves and has a diamond ring.

21″ #2193, 1969 brown-eyed, brown-haired Melanie wears a strapless dress of blue faille cut on the princess style with gathers at back waistline. Her matching jacket is trimmed with white braid and lace trims the sleeves and around the neck ending at the waistline. Her matching poke bonnet is brightened with tiny flowers and is tied under her chin with a satin ribbon. Her undergarments consist of heavy net-lined crinoline slip, white taffeta pantaloons trimmed at the ankles with lace and blue ribbon. Her only jewelry is a diamond ring.

21″ #2190. 1969. Green-eyed, brunette Scarlett, wears a green taffeta square-neck, sleeveless dress with armholes of white lace that match the lace on the full-length sleeves of the jacket. Jacket and skirt are both trimmed with green and white braid. The braid is in sharp peaks on the skirt. Her matching poke bonnet features a spray of apple blossoms and lavender flowers. Her undergarments consist of stiff material formed in the shape of panniers snapped on separately from a half slip of net-lined crinoline. She wears cotton pantaloons trimmed with eyelet lace with green ribbon inserts, stockings and black sling-back shoes. Her jewelry is a gold heart-shaped locket with one rhinestone set and a diamond ring.

21" Renoir, 1969, #2194 is a beautiful blue-eyed brunette wearing a white lace over yellow taffeta gown. The skirt features a deep flounce and her waist is encircled with a bright yellow taffeta ribbon. The back has a full two-layered bustle with two streamers of yellow taffeta approximately 7" wide. The long sleeves are trimmed with white lace matching the trim on the high neckline. Her natural straw hat is rolled at the edge and trimmed with yellow tulle and small velvet violets. The dress features an attached slip lined with yellow taffeta. Under this she wears a heavy crinoline, net-lined slip with full attached flounce. Her pantaloons are trimmed at the ankles with yellow ribbon through eyelet lace. Her shoes are gold sling-backs. Her jewelry consists of double-drop pearl earrings, cameo necklace encircled with rhinestones and a diamond ring.

21″ #2196, 1970 Melanie has brown eyes and brunette hair which is pulled to the sides with four long curls. Her beautiful white, dotted swiss dress consists of three tiers. Each tier is trimmed with white lace threaded with red ribbon and matching the trim of the v-neckline and the edge of the sleeves. Her undergarments are white net-lined crinoline with white lace trim at bottom edge, white taffeta pantaloons trimmed with red eyelet lace and red ribbon. Her white picture hat is trimmed with white net, large, red roses and small, blue flowers. Melanie carries a red cotton umbrella trimmed with white lace and wears a cameo necklace encircled with rhinestones and a diamond ring.

#2197, 1970 Madame Pompadour is dressed in pink satin with overskirt panniers of pink brocade matching the bodice and sleeves of the dress. The neckline is trimmed in pink lace and tiny rosettas of blue, pink, yellow and lavender. These rosettas also decorate the scalloped edges of the panniers. Madame wears a pink ostrich feather in her puffed hair. Undergarments consist of pink net-lined crinoline with pink lace at bottom edge. She wears pink taffeta pantaloons with pink trim at the ankles and pink, sling-back shoes. She wears a lone, large rhinestone necklace, drop rhinestone clustered earrings, and a diamond ring. In her right hand she carries a lace fan.

21″ #2195, 1970 Godey with ash-blonde hair and blue eyes is dressed in pink ribbon, satin trimmed with beige lace at neckline, down front of bodice and on edge of full-length sleeves. The cape-jacket is of deep lavender and fastened in the front with a lavender stone pin. Her hat is fashioned of lilac net with tiny lavender flowers. Her slip is pink, net-lined crinoline. Her pantaloons are deep pink with matching lace trim. She wears pink sling-back shoes, pearl double-drop earrings and a diamond ring.

21″ #2180, 1970 Scarlett, a green-eyed brunette wears a green taffeta, square-neck, sleeveless dress with arm-holes of white lace that matches the lace on the full-length sleeves of the jacket. Jacket and skirt are both trimmed with green and white braid. The braid on the skirt forms scallops. Her matching poke bonnet features pink flowers. Her undergarments consist of stiff mate-rial in the shape of panniers snapped on separately from a half slip of net-lined crinoline. She wears cotton pantaloons trimmed with eyelet lace and emerald green ribbon. She wears black sling-backs. Her jewelry is a gold heart-shaped locket with one rhinestone and a dia-mond ring.

14" — 1970 Jenny Lind in pink satin formal. Lace trims the skirt and bodice of her gown. She wears flowers in her hair and three tiny rosettas trim along lace of the skirt.

21" — #2181, 1970 Jenny Lind is as shown. The main difference between the 1969 and the 1970 is the lace edging on the panniers. This doll had the lace added to a 1969 Portrait and was offered to me as a 1970 doll.

21″ #2162, 1971 Melanie, with blue eyes and red hair wears a strapless gown of heavy blue taffeta, cut on princess lines. A matching strolling-length coat is trimmed with white sequins at sleeve edge and forming a loop at corner. She wears white, net-lined crinoline slip, white pantaloons with blue ribbon trim at ankles and white sling-back shoes. A cameo necklace encircled with rhinestones and a diamond ring complete her ensemble.

21″ #2161, 1971 blue-eyed, blonde Godey is dressed in a strapless gown of pink satin trimmed with black braid and two panels of embroidered black tape. Her black velvet jacket is trimmed at sleeve and jacket edge with rainbow-colored sequins. Godey's bonnet is of matching black velvet with pink rosebuds across the edge and a satin ribbon tying under the chin. She wears a pink net-lined crinoline slip, pink pantaloons, and matching sling-back shoes. Her jewelry consists of a cameo necklace and a diamond ring.

21″ #2163, 1971 Renoir, a brown-eyed brunette, is dressed in a gorgeous two-piece yellow taffeta dress. The skirt is accordian pleated. The dress top consists of long sleeves trimmed with yellow lace matching lace at neckline. Also trimmed with sequins starting at shoulder, going down to waist, across to opposite side and up to shoulder seam matching one row of sequins at center front of bodice. Sequins also trim the edge of the waist. Renoir wears white net-lined crinoline slip with white taffeta pantaloons trimmed with lace and yellow satin ribbon. She has gold sling-back shoes. Her natural straw hat is encircled with yellow tulle and topped with a circle of all-colored flowers. She wears double-drop pearl earrings, a cameo and rhinestone necklace and a diamond ring.

21″ #2170, 1971 Mimi was made only one y↓ar. With blonde hair and blue eyes, she is dressed in a white taffeta, sleeveless gown with a rose pink cape-coat lined with white taffeta. The dress is trimmed with rose-pink braid. Her rose pink hat is trimmed with white and pink field flowers that matches the tulle of her neck scarf. White net lines her crinoline slip, and she wears white pantaloons with pink ribbon and lace trim at ankles. She has white sling-back shoes, rhinestone drop earrings, a teardrop rhinestone necklace and a diamond ring.

21″ #2191, 1972 Cornelia with blonde hair and blue eyes, is dressed in a hot pink sleeveless gown and matching cape-coat. The sleeve edge is trimmed with white lace and the dress is trimmed with a white braid scroll. She wears a white crinoline slip, white taffeta pantaloons, stockings, and pink sling-back shoes.

21″ #2190, 1972 Renoir is blue-eyed and blonde. Renoir's dress is bright-pink; skirt trimmed in black braid with high neckline trimmed with pink lace and matching lace down center front of bodice. The black velvet jacket is trimmed with bright sequins around edge of jacket and sleeves. Renoir's hat is of pink taffeta with matching tulle trim and small rosebuds. (Note: the satin in this dress is very thin in comparison with other satin and there is no tulle tie under the chin.) She wears white taffeta pantaloons, white net-lined crinoline, stockings and black sling-back shoes. She has a rhinestone brooch at neck and a diamond ring.

21″ #2192, 1972 Gainsborough is a dark, ash blonde beautifully dressed in a gown of bright blue in the same style as Renoir 1969 and 1970. Her undergarments are a net-lined crinoline, white taffeta pantaloons edged with blue ribbon at ankles, stockings and blue sling-back shoes. She wears a plain heart-shaped locket, a diamond ring and double pearl earrings. Her hat is of natural straw pulled up on one side with blue tulle and caught with a pink rose and buds.

21″ Cornelia, #2191, 1973, is a green-eyed brunette wearing a deep-pink taffeta dress with matching tunic coat trimmed with beige lace at neckline and sleeve edge. Soutache braid trim brings the length of her coat into focus. She has matching sling-back shoes, and stockings. Her brimmed hat is trimmed with gold tulle and violet buds. She has a gold heart-shaped locket and a sparkling ring on her finger.

21″ #2192, 1973 Gainsborough is an auburn-haired, blue-eyed beauty wearing a pale-blue satin gown with overskirt. The scalloped edge is caught up with rose bud trim and worn over a tulle-pleated, pale-blue skirt. A matching hat with blue tulle trim, and rosebuds have tulle streamers which tie under her chin. Her undergarments are white taffeta pantaloons with lace and blue ribbon trim and matching blue sling-back shoes. She has a cameo pendant and a ring on her finger. It is interesting to note a store price tag of $55.

21″ Renoir, #2190, 1973 is a honey blonde with brown eyes in a gold long-sleeved dress with rhinestone buttons down the front of bodice. Her dress is trimmed with matching ruffle at bottom and second ruffle in front forming "apron" at back. She has stockings and gold sling-back shoes. Renoir is wearing a natural straw hat trimmed with tulle and flowers. She wears a sparkling ring on her finger.

21″ — #2297, 1974 Agatha is dressed in a pale-pink dress with matching cape-coat with mother-of-pearl braid down front to and around hemline. Rosebuds trim the neckline. Undergarments consist of matching pale-pink slip, pantaloons, and pink sling-back shoes. She is wearing a seed pearl necklace and a sparkling ring.

21″ Cornelia, #2296, 1974. Our blue-eyed, auburn-haired beauty looks charming in her powder-blue, silk dress and matching three-quarter length coat trimmed in pale-blue lace at neck and sleeve edge. Black braid trim on edges of coat form loops at corners. Her bonnet is blue taffeta with black lace and rosebuds. A heavy crinoline slip, white taffeta pantaloons and black sling-back shoes are her undergarments. She is wearing a cameo necklace and a sparkling ring on her finger.

21″ Melanie, #2295, 1974 is a very much desired doll because of the striking white and bright-red ensemble. Melanie is a brown-eyed brunette wearing full white-pleated dress. A bright-red jacket with white lace at sleeve edge and on bodice of dress are part of her ensemble. A poke bonnet with red trim matches her jacket. She wears a white crinoline slip, white taffeta pantaloons, stockings and red sling-back shoes. A ring on her finger is her only jewelry.

21″ #2290, 1975 Cornelia is blonde and blue-eyed and dressed in a beautiful shocking-pink moire taffeta dress and matching three-quarter length coat trimmed with black braid and beige lace on cuff and down front of the coat. Her hat is made of black tulle with red roses for trim. Streamers from the hat tie under the chin. Undergarments are a white net-lined crinoline and white taffeta pantaloons both trimmed with red satin ribbon interlaced in eyelet lace, stockings and black sling-back shoes. Her jewelry is a cameo necklace encircled with rhinestones and a sparkling ring.

21″ #2291, 1975, Agatha with blue eyes and honey-blonde hair is wearing a pale-blue taffeta dress with mother-of-pearl trim. White lace edges the cuffs and the front of the dress. Her matching poke bonnet is trimmed on each side with blue ribbon rosettes and ties under her chin in a bow. She is wearing a net-lined crinoline trimmed at the hemline with blue interlacing ribbon, white pantaloons trimmed to match hemline of slip, stockings and white sling-back shoes. Her jewelry is a lone sparkling ring.

21″ #2292, 1975, Scarlett, with her green eyes and long brunette hair is wearing an emerald green sleeveless dress, and a jacket trimmed with contrasting braid and white lace. Her pantaloons are white taffeta trimmed with green satin ribbons. She wears stockings, sling-back shoes, a cameo encircled with rhinestones and a diamond ring. Her poke bonnet matches the dress and ties under the chin in a bow.

21″ #2293, 1976, Cornelia is blonde and blue-eyed and beautifully fits the description of Cornelia 1976. She is dressed in an unusually soft rose pink taffeta, trimmed with a beautiful patterned design of black sequins entwined with pink braid giving the illusion of a coat. The front of the bodice and sleeve edge are trimmed with lace matching her dress. Her hat is made of tulle, picking up the color of the braid trim and tying under the chin in a large bow. Pink roses are the only hat trim. Lace and ribbon edge the slip and pantaloons. She wears long stockings and black sling-back shoes. Her jewelry consists of a cameo necklace and a ring. Her tag reads "Agatha."

21″ #2294, 1976 Agatha with blue eyes and auburn hair is dressed in an aqua-blue taffeta gown with matching three-quarter length coat trimmed with white silver braid and white lace. A lovely seed pearl pin closes the coat. Her matching poke bonnet is trimmed with lace and braid and ties under her chin with a large ribbon bow. Matching blue ribbon and lace trimmed the slip and pantaloons, stockings, and blue sling shoes. She wears a cameo necklace and a sparkling ring on her finger. Her dress tag reads "Cornelia" which I am sure is a factory error as the description fits that of Agatha in the catalog.

21" #2297, 1977, Magnolia is a new name in Alexander portraits. Magnolia wears a soft, pink taffeta gown, high-styled with an insert of 13 rows of matching lace over taffeta. Matching lace trims the sleeve edge, neckline and from each shoulder seam ending in a v at waistline. White net lines the pink crinoline slip also trimmed in pink lace as are the taffeta pantaloons. She wears stockings and pink sling-back shoes. A ring and a lone opal pendant are her jewelry. Her auburn-red hair is protected with a pink sheer picture hat trimmed at crown with flowers and ribbon. It is tied under the chin with a satin bow.

21" #2298 1977 Godey with blonde hair and blue eyes, is dressed in a taffeta sleeveless dress and a red velvet jacket. The jacket is trimmed with matching braid and closed at the waistline with a hook and eye. Beige lace trims the sleeve and neck edge. The skirt of her dress is trimmed with white braid in a swirl design on each side of center. She wears net-lined crinoline and taffeta pantaloons trimmed with white lace. Her shoes are pink sling backs and her jewelry is a "ruby" pendent and a "diamond" ring. Her blonde hair is highlighted by a bright-red taffeta hat trimmed with field flowers across the crown.

21″ — 1978 Scarlett

21″ — 1978 Gainsborgho

Shari #2430, 21″ and 14″. Shari wears a gold bouffant skirt of gold lace, fully lined and worn with a matching blouse top, with imported braid trimming the bodice front and the edge of the three-fourths length sleeve. She wears a pink taffeta belt and a spray of pink roses. Our girls both wear yellow crinolines and yellow taffeta panties, nylon stockings and gold sandals. Shari wears a gold ball necklace and a gold bracelet and pearl earrings. Both 14 and 21-inch Sharis wear roses in their hair.

Shari Lewis was well known star of television. 1959

14″ Shari Lewis, 1959, #2431. Shari is dressed in rose pink polished cotton fashioned into a shirtwaist dress. Around her waist she wears a gold belt with three gold balls on it. A tiny rhinestone trims the cuff of her three-fourths length sleeve. To complete her ensemble, she wears a natural straw, wide-brimmed hat with a black velvet ribbon and the crown encircled with field flowers. She wears pink high-heeled sandals and her only jewelry is a pair of drop pearl earrings.

1959, 21″ Shari, #1432. Shari wears a teal-blue dress with bracelet-length sleeves and a wide silver belt in shirtwaist fashion, silver shoes, a solitaire ring, pearl earrings, and a large, natural straw hat trimmed with pink flowers.

21″ — Shari Lewis, 1959, #2433, with one-piece graceful arms Shari wears a skirt of emerald-green slipper satin and a jersey blouse of yellow. Her contour belt of gold draws attention to her tiny waistline. She wears a yellow crinoline slip with an additional nylon net ruffle. Her large, green straw hat with bright pink flowers is matched to her double-strand green beads encircling her neck. An emerald-green solitaire ring, and a pendant watch pinned to the waistline of her skirt, pearl earrings, and green, high-heeled sandals complete her ensemble.

16″ — #1895-1959. Sleeping Beauty. Jointed at elbows, knees and ankles. Rhinestones in crown and ring. Also, a rhinestone necklace. Gold high heel shoes. She has gold tag at waist saying — "Sleeping Beauty Walt Dis-ney Prod." On back of tag reads "Madame Alexander presents Walt Disney's Authentic Sleeping Beauty." Courtesy — Roberta Lago.

21″ — Sleeping Beauty, #2195. Walt Disney's Sleeping Beauty brought to reality by Madame Alexander dressed beautifully in soft-blue satin trimmed with gold. Her long golden curls touch her waistline in back. Her golden tiara, with rhinestones makes her look like a princess. She wears a golden cape of brocaded net. She wears a rhinestone necklace and a ring.

Sleeping Beauty, 10 inch (Cissette), 1960 #795, all original.

That Girl, Marlo Thomas, the prize-winning TV show on the ABC network gives us "That Girl," Marlo Thomas, the star. The much-loved show inspired this 17″ girl doll. Marlo, #1793, in a soft jersey shift dress in royal blue and green worn with a choker necklace. Wearing white lace stockings and white high-heeled boots, she is up front in the fashion of today. 1967. Courtesy of Mary Pattom.

The "First Ladies" 1976 14″ *Left to right* — Martha Washington #1501, Abigail Adams #1502, Martha Randolf #1503.

*Left to right* — Dolly Madison #1504, Elizabeth Monroe #1505, and Louisa Adams # 1506.

# INDEX